Alina Tofan

The role of the external factor in the political process of the Kyrgyz Republic

Alina Tofan

The role of the external factor in the political process of the Kyrgyz Republic

ScienciaScripts

Imprint

Any brand names and product names mentioned in this book are subject to trademark, brand or patent protection and are trademarks or registered trademarks of their respective holders. The use of brand names, product names, common names, trade names, product descriptions etc. even without a particular marking in this work is in no way to be construed to mean that such names may be regarded as unrestricted in respect of trademark and brand protection legislation and could thus be used by anyone.

Cover image: www.ingimage.com

This book is a translation from the original published under ISBN 978-3-659-58376-6.

Publisher:
Sciencia Scripts
is a trademark of
Dodo Books Indian Ocean Ltd. and OmniScriptum S.R.L publishing group

120 High Road, East Finchley, London, N2 9ED, United Kingdom
Str. Armeneasca 28/1, office 1, Chisinau MD-2012, Republic of Moldova, Europe
Printed at: see last page
ISBN: 978-620-7-97308-8

TABLE OF CONTENTS:

CHAPTER 1

CENTRAL ASIA AS AN OBJECT OF GEOPOLITICAL COMPETITION BETWEEN GLOBAL PLAYERS

"The processes taking place in the post-Soviet space can be called one of the central planks of contemporary world politics. It is one of its most dynamic, dramatic and sharp south with a multitude of lines and multidirectional vectors, a complex interweaving of heterogeneous forces and factors, instability and contradictory trends. It is also where most of the major phenomena, painful issues and contradictions of the modern stage of history are reflected and intertwined"[1] , - this thesis by E.A. Narochnitskaya characterises the specifics of the current political conjuncture in the post-Soviet space and in Central Asia in particular.

Central Asia is a median geopolitical space that has traditionally been important both globally and regionally. For many centuries, the Central Asian region has played a leading role in world politics, and by now its importance has been further enhanced. Occupying a strategic geopolitical position, being at the crossroads of civilisations, possessing the richest natural resources and advantageous transport routes and communications, the region is a concentration of vital interests of the West, the East and Russia. The English geographer and geopolitician X. Mackinder argued that hegemony over the world is possible only if control over Eurasia, of which the Central Asian region is a part - the World Island, the heart of which is the Heartland (the territory from the Volga to the Yangtze, from the Himalayas to the Arctic): "Whoever controls Europe commands the Heartland; whoever controls the Heartland commands the World Island, whoever controls the World Island commands the world."[2]

Due to its uniqueness, the Central Asian region is an object of concentration of not only geopolitical but also economic interests of various powers. The economic attractiveness of Central Asia is represented by significant reserves of natural resources. Central Asia is an important reserve for the diversification of hydrocarbons and its transport routes. This is another aspect of why Central Asian countries attract the attention of world powers. For Russia, Central Asia is also important because the security of its oil and gas exports is directly dependent on the border countries through which energy resources transit.

---

[1] *Narochnitskaya E.A.* Post-Soviet space in the world mosaic and US strategy *And* http://www. perspektivy. mfo/book/postsovetskoje prostranstvo v mirovoj mozaike i strategii ssha 2008- 05-15.htm

[2] *Trifkovic S.* Geopolitics of the New Multipolarity. Conference at the IJU, 27 May 2014 // http://www.idc-europe.org/ru/-Геополитика-новой-мультиполярности-

Central Asia today appears as a place of concentration of various global, regional, as well as numerous bilateral interests, is the object of close attention of modern centres of power, which automatically makes its partners not only border states, but also quite distant states. In the global world, this separateness does not exist: major powers are able to exert their influence and generate powerful impulses in politics and economy practically in any corner of the globe.

Over the past few decades, the geopolitical picture in Central Asia has undergone a number of qualitative changes. Since about 2001, the United States has been conquering free niches, not only without resistance but, moreover, with the consent of the states themselves. We can state the fact that the era of unlimited Russian dominance in the region is coming to an end. New geopolitical players have emerged in the region, who insistently defend their interests, not always considering (or not considering at all) the opinion of Russian diplomacy.

The competition between the West, represented by the United States, and Russia over Central Asia can be called a competition between Western and Eurasian civilisations. It should be emphasised that it is the United States that represents Western civilisation. Today, the European Union is completely dependent on Washington - it is an American satellite, which has no opportunity to conduct its foreign policy sovereignly and decide important issues independently.

The EU will gain sovereignty only after the relations between Washington and Brussels change dramatically. However, today Europe follows the US in many aspects. Such external governance is explained by the fact that the power today is held by financial elites closely linked to the U.S. Federal Reserve System, which, of course, pursue a policy aimed solely at realising their own interests. The industrial elites of the European Union, which are more interested in co-operation with the post-Soviet states, are in a subordinate position in relation to them.

Thus, by extending the zones of vital interests of the USA to the scale of the whole planet, and the content of these interests - to the control over natural, demographic and economic resources of other countries, as well as by fixing the exclusive monopoly on the use of force in international affairs for the American military-diplomatic machine, the USA ensures its dominant position in the world, backed by the unparalleled US military-industrial complex.

The United States is a superpower that plays an independent decisive role in world politics, overshadowing the legal formalities of existing models of international law, and seeks to establish a certain model of world politics and ensure total control over political processes around the world, including the post-Soviet space.

Russia is developing its own alternative to Atlanticism - Eurasianism, a supranational strategic alliance of countries and cultures living on a single continent and united by a common historical mission, designed to clash with the impending "world order" under the aegis of the United States.

It should be noted that the political elites of the Central Asian states have also often contributed to the intensification of Russian-American competition in the region in order to realise their own economic or political interests, as well as to strengthen their own positions of power by clashing Moscow and Washington. This occurs both as a result of day-to-day official interactions, when state leaders try to manoeuvre through the rivalry between Moscow and Washington, and at specific moments when states change the direction of their foreign policy in order to gain both political patronage and material assistance. An example is Uzbekistan, which changes its foreign policy orientation time after time, either joining the CSTO or becoming a member of GUAM. The democratism of post-Soviet states is quite often nothing more than a political way of settling their internal issues with the help of US material resources.

The leaders of the region's states often use relations with the EU and the US as a tool to pressure the Russian Federation for their own benefit. It can also be seen that the intensification of relations between the US and the EU on the one hand and the states of the region on the other is almost always accompanied by a deterioration of relations between Russia and the EU with the US.

For the US, the so-called "Central Eurasian regional pentagon" - Central Eastern Europe and the Balkans - the Caucasus - Central Asia - the Middle East - the Middle East - is strategically important.[3]

The United States is making maximum efforts to gain a strong foothold in Central Asia, because US dominance in Eurasia actually means the establishment of unipolarity in international relations, which the Russian Federation should not categorically allow. A. Arsenenko, a Russian researcher, called the US policy in the post-Soviet space "a crusade of

---

[3] See: *Shmakov I.* US offensive in the post-Soviet space // http://www.posprikaz.ru/ 2012/03/ nastuplenie-ssha-na-postsovetskom-prostranstve/.

US imperialism against the former Soviet republics".[4]

Another goal of the policy pursued by the US is to "squeeze" Russia out of the post-Soviet space, since without the latter it is virtually impossible to consider Russia as a serious geopolitical player.

Here we should pay special attention to the fact that the USA realises not only and not so much its own national interests, but also the interests of various transnational corporations, which have long taken a firm place among the leading subjects of world historical and political processes, are the main determinant of international relations, world politics and economy, being the main source of capital flow in the form of direct investments.

At the same time, it should be noted that the main goal of modern American MNCs is to increase the market rather than to increase profits. TNCs need a favourable investment climate in the region, in particular, a favourable economic position, protection of investors' interests, financial, tax and other advantages, which is achieved through the creation of puppet governments financed and subsidised by these corporations themselves in the person of the United States. American transnational corporations have assigned the Central Asian States the role of a so-called raw materials appendage.

It is interesting to note that this strategy began to be used in the years after World War II, when the U.S. Foreign Affairs Council presented the concept of "Big Zone Planning," where a "big zone" is an area "strategically necessary for world control. So, in this case, Central Asia is precisely this "big zone".

Speaking about the tools used by the United States to pursue its strategic interests, it should be noted that the U.S. foreign policy has several stages. The preparatory stage is based on offensive methods of influence.

Thus, if a state declares its neutral position towards the United States, then, firstly, the U.S. authorities place the main emphasis in their diplomacy on the violation of human rights in this country. Next, the state is invited to cooperate with the aim of stabilising the situation with respect to democratic principles. If the foreign policy of the state changes positively towards the USA, then Washington's actions change. Accusations at the state level of human rights violations are replaced by statements about "improvement" of the situation in this sphere. The third stage is the deployment of US military bases on the territory of a given state.

---

[4] *Arseenko A.* How US imperialism "grinds" the post-Soviet space // http://left.ru/2007/17/arseenko169.phtml

The US military presence on the territory of a state requires not only a pro-American regime, but also a pro-American elite and, even better, its proxies in power. Finally, the fourth stage is the stage of consolidating its presence. At this stage, accusations of violation of human rights and freedoms are again made, and US diplomatic agencies begin to form a "democratic opposition" whose task will be to finally strengthen the US position in the state in question.[5] "The Washington Post once wrote that "the U.S. must act more vigorously to stop the erosion of democracy.[6]

S. Talbot, former First Deputy Secretary of State of the United States, outlined four areas that the United States uses as mechanisms of "soft power". These are, firstly, the promotion and development of democracy and the formation of civil society. Secondly, the creation of a free market economy and the stimulation and forcing of privatisation processes. Thirdly, helping to resolve conflicts that could undermine regional stability. And finally, to promote the integration of small states in the region into the world community.[7]

An interesting point of view of some researchers is that the methods of implementation of the US policy in Central Asia are similar to the methods of the Nazi Germany leadership as set out in the General Plan "Ost", with which the intentions of destroying Russian statehood, fragmentation of the USSR and isolation of the Union republics using the principle of "divide and rule" are connected[8] .

It should be noted here that the U.S. objective is not simply to neutralise "Russian imperialism", but to eliminate the possibility of a counterweight to the U.S. by bringing Western standards of democracy and market reforms to the Central Asian states. Some U.S. policymakers believe that Russia's presence in the Central Asian states could negatively affect the potential for democratic transformation in these states and undermine their sovereignty.[9]

Russia, in response to the US desire to change the priorities of the domestic and foreign policies of the Central Asian states, has no choice but to take the position of a stabiliser of the situation in the states. At the same time, it should be emphasised that the Russian Federation

---

[5] See: *Moshkina V*. Russian-American competition in Central Asia / Collection of scientific articles "Central Asian region: modern political and socio-economic dynamics" - B., 2011. - C. 120.

[6] *Shchukin D*. Western wind for the Middle East storm. What variant of the world order can Russia offer today? // http://www.centrasia.ru/newsA.php?st=1299056460

[7] See: *Ziegler* C US Strategy in Central Asia and the SCO / MEMO. - 2005. - № 4. - C. 14.

[8] See: *Dashichev V.* US policy in the post-Soviet space in historical comparisons // http://www.km.ru/spetsproekty/2011/06/25/istoriya-sssr/amerikanskaya-politika-na-postsovetskom- prostranstve-v-istoric

[9] See: *Trotsky M., Charap S.* Russian-American relations in the post-Soviet space. How to overcome the zero-sum game? / Reports of the Working Group on the Future of Russian-American Relations. - 2011. - № 1. - C. 15.

is realising its national interests exclusively. A significant means by which Russia can increase its influence and strengthen its presence in the context of geopolitical competition with the United States is the so-called "structural block creation", i.e. the creation of various integration associations and unions with the aim of uniting various groups of post-Soviet states. Such associations could be the Customs Union and the Eurasian Economic Space with the prospect of growing into the Eurasian Economic Union, whose members would significantly strengthen their positions in the face of the rest of the world community. [10]

Thus, countering aggressive anti-Atlanticism, Russia uses rather soft, but at the same time effective methods:

1) maintaining military and political alliances and attempting to create new alliances;

2) Use of economic methods of co-operation

3) spreading influence through integration structures (Customs Union).

In an attempt to hold Central Asia and the post-Soviet space in general, Russian diplomats developed the principle of "mobile geometry", which is actively used today, thanks to which the post-Soviet states, taking into account their political, economic, strategic and other interests, can sign interstate agreements and treaties with the possibility of reservations and taking into account their own dissenting opinions.

It should be noted that the US presence in Central Asia and its competition with Russia does not bring any positive transformations as a result. "A policy based on the notion of competition between the US and Russia also hampers the political and economic development of post-Soviet Eurasia and contributes to the "freezing" of unresolved conflicts. Thus, the unrest in Kyrgyzstan in early 2010 was largely caused by Moscow's and Washington's actions towards Bishkek. The U.S. and Russia were not shy to engage in unseemly bargaining for the right to deploy a military base in the country. This only served to strengthen the power of an extremely corrupt and unpopular clique among the Kyrgyz. In addition to Kyrgyzstan, a prime example is Ukraine, where the perception of an acute rivalry between the U.S. and Russia has deepened the cultural and linguistic divide in society, making it difficult for all Ukrainian citizens to achieve national self-determination". [11]

---

[10] See: *Larin A.G.* Towards the assessment of China's economic activities in the post-Soviet space in the light of Russian interests // http://www.ifes-ras.ru/publications/monograph/591_-k-oczenke-ekonomicheskoj_-_deyatelnosti-kitaya-na-postsovetskom-prostranstve-v-svete-rossijskix-interesov

[11] *Trotsky M., Charap S.* Russian-American relations in the post-Soviet space. How to overcome the zero-sum game? / Reports of the Working Group on the Future of U.S.-Russian Relations. - 2011. - № 1. - C. 18.

The tilting of the foreign policy vectors of the Central Asian states towards the United States or Russia entails significant internal political changes. The first phase of relations between the Central Asian states and the United States covers the years 1991-1995, i.e. from the time of independence. This phase is characterised by a minimal level of US involvement in the region's internal processes. At this stage, the main U.S. positions on Central Asia are defined, and the institutional basis for U.S. participation in reforming the political, economic and social spheres in the states of the region is formed. During this period, Central Asia occupies one of the last places in the US foreign policy strategy.

The change comes from 1995, when the United States included the region in the sphere of its political, economic and military interests. The second stage of CA-US relations (1995-1999) is characterised by active US entry into Central Asia through international financial institutions and US-controlled military-political blocs. At this stage, the United States formed a pro-American lobby in the states of the region, providing citizens with the opportunity to participate in educational programmes, attracting Central Asian states to participate in Western economic and political organisations and actively supporting the leadership of the republics in this direction. In particular, through the world financial institutions, as well as on a bilateral basis, the USA began to impose on the governments of the states of the region the mechanical transfer of liberal market models without taking into account internal peculiarities, which, for example, for Kyrgyzstan, resulted in widespread privatisation, collapse of the industrial complex inherited from the USA, destruction of the real sector of the economy and loss of economic ties with the Russian Federation.

In addition, the U.S. began active preferential lending to the economies of the region, which in fact replaced the practice of subsidising the economies from the centre during the Soviet era. At the same time, the aim of reforming the economies was not to expand trade and economic ties with the region, but to financially exploit the republics through a system of preferential lending. As a result, the US began to determine the key vectors of fiscal and monetary policy in the Central Asian states. The growing financial dependence on the US made the economically weak states of the region hostage to US political and military interests.

Since 2000, the United States has been even more active in influencing internal processes in the region. The third stage of relations (2000-2010) is defined by the widespread penetration of the United States in Central Asia. The US declares its responsibility for democratisation, security and stability of the region, establishes political regimes controlled by Washington, and consolidates its military and political presence, thus implementing its project to establish world domination.[12] The development of the US-Uzbekistan partnership has led to an increase in anti-Russian rhetoric, and the Uzbek authorities have decided to replace the Russian Federation as the main supplier of weapons to the RU army. In 2001 Uzbekistan made its territory available to host a US military airbase. In April 2002, UZ President Karimov I. emphasised that the U.S. had actively contributed to and played a decisive role in defusing tensions in the south of the republic. At the same time, he emphasised that the participants in the CST had not proved themselves in any way. Active cooperation between Uzbekistan and the U.S. continued until 2005, when the Uzbek leadership accused Western organisations and the U.S. government of organising the unrest in Andijan. Uzbekistan curtailed co-operation with the U.S. and passed a law terminating the Karshi-Khanabad base. In the same period, a US Air Force base was opened in the Kyrgyz Republic, where it existed until 2014 and was repeatedly the subject of bargaining between the government of the Kyrgyz Republic on the one hand and the leadership of the US and the Russian Federation on the other.

Thus, with the help of "soft power" and further "humanitarian intervention" the US turns states from political subjects into objects of its geopolitical game. This often affects states with weak sovereignty and corrupt elites capable of violating national security and state interests in favour of selfish personal interests.

The most favourable position in this situation is found in states that possess a significant amount of natural resources and, therefore, have sufficient means to independently regulate their own economies. For example, Turkmenistan, which has significant natural gas reserves, has been able to maintain its foreign policy neutrality and, to date, has not allowed Western companies to develop its fields. Kazakhstan, which has 96 per cent of the region's total oil reserves, is also increasing its national stake in oil projects, which in the 1990s were transferred on favourable terms to Western companies.

With the beginning of Donald Trump's presidency, Washington's policy towards Central Asia has changed somewhat. The US plans to stop financial injections into Kazakhstan and Turkmenistan, significantly reduce financial support to Kyrgyzstan and Tajikistan, and only slightly increase subsidies to Uzbekistan.[13]

---

[12] See: *Omarov N.M.* Foreign policy of the Kyrgyz Republic in the era of "strategic uncertainty". - Б., 2005. - С. 165.
[13] See: Vorobyev A. Not One Way: The Interests of the PRC and the Russian Federation in Central Asia //

Since the beginning of the 21st century, with the coming to power of V.V. Putin, a revision of Russia's foreign policy towards Central Asia has begun. The Russian Federation's foreign policy towards Central Asia has been undergoing a revision since the beginning of the 21st century. It began to intensify co-operation with Central Asian states not only in political, but also in military, economic and social spheres. In autumn 2003, a Russian air base began its deployment in Kyrgyzstan, and in 2004 a military base was established in Tajikistan, which confirmed the Russian Federation's intentions of strategic presence in the region. In addition, since the early 2000s, economic ties between the Russian Federation and the states of the region began to grow, which initially led to an increase in the share of Russian capital in the economy of the Central Asian states, and subsequently to the formation of the Customs Union between Russia, Belarus and Kazakhstan and Kyrgyzstan's further accession to it. [14]

At the same time, it should be noted that Kazakhstan has steadily oriented its foreign policy aspirations towards the Russian Federation, with a diametrically opposite situation to that of its neighbours in the region. Kazakhstan, a reliable political ally, which insists on Eurasianism, supports post-Soviet integration, and founded the Customs Union and the Eurasian Economic Union, is characterised by its leading position in Central Asia and stable economic growth.

Central Asia's cooperation with Russia is also attractive from an ideological point of view: the Russian project of democratising the region assumes that the leadership of the republics will independently determine the timing and scope of the transformation of their political systems, taking into account regional specificities and without external interference. [15]

Thus, the competition for Central Asia is unfolding between two strong players - Russia and the United States, Eurasianism and the West. The Central Asian states in this competition are the objects of the foreign policy of these powers, not only not forming their own political vectors, but also forced to choose the models of co-operation from those offered. The difference in the methods and tools of this competition demonstrates the actual attitude

---

http://expert.ru/2017/07/3/kitaj -i-tsentralnaya-aziya/

[14] See: *Ormonova A.A.* Cooperation between Russia and Kyrgyzstan in the sphere of economy: history of the issue / Bulletin of A.S. Pushkin Leningrad State University. - 2014. - № 1. - T. 6. - C. 77.

[15] See: *Muratalieva 3.* Kyrgyzstan is turning into a hostage of geopolitical confrontation between China and Russia // https://regnum.ru/news/1866113.html

of these powers to the newly independent states - the aggressive strategy of the United States is opposed by rather mild models of cooperation offered by Russia, since due to historical peculiarities Russia's presence in the region is not realised at all through forceful coercion. The result of this competition is the splitting of the formerly integral region, and in this situation, the main task that Russia must face is to prevent U.S. interference in the internal political affairs of the Central Asian states, to overcome this split, to unite the space under the ideology of Eurasianism, and to restore the balance of power in international relations. This is the only way to prevent the pervasive all-pervasive hegemony of the United States aimed at building a unipolar world.

CHAPTER 2

STRATEGIC INTERESTS OF THE USA, RUSSIA AND CHINA IN THE KYRGYZ REPUBLIC

The Kyrgyz Republic is a state that, due to its geographical location and loyal foreign policy course, has become an arena of clashing interests of the world's political players. Kyrgyzstan is a part of Central Asia, which is geographically a key region on the political map of the world, a foothold in which makes it possible to control the transit of hydrocarbons and other strategic resources; Central Asia is a kind of crossroads of Western and Eastern civilisations, the establishment of control over which will make it possible to establish control over almost the entire world.

Due to the fact that after the collapse of the USSR Kyrgyzstan faced a huge number of internal problems, which were previously solved by subsidies from above, in the absence of natural resources or the difficulty of their extraction, the profit from the sale of which could become a source of replenishment of the state budget, Kyrgyzstan began to actively seek foreign policy allies, patrons who would be able to credit the economy, allowing the newly independent state to stay afloat. At the same time, the republic did not build a clear foreign policy course, preferring to talk about multi-vector policy, which brought to Kyrgyzstan rival geopolitical players with completely opposite interests, goals and strategies. Today, Kyrgyzstan, taking advantage of its convenient geographical location (being in Central Asia and directly bordering China), is trying to balance the interests of three key global players: the United States, the Russian Federation and China.

Since 1991, the United States has been actively involved in the domestic political processes in the Kyrgyz Republic: through global financial institutions, it has provided loans to the economy and participated in the reform of the political and economic systems. In general, however, US economic interests in Kyrgyzstan are less significant than political interests. Trade turnover between the countries is insignificant, and American investments in the Kyrgyz economy are minimal. However, U.S. involvement in domestic political processes is indisputable: through non-governmental organisations, the United States interfered in the electoral process, managed to carry out a "colour revolution", and stationed a military base on the territory of the republic. Over the years of bilateral co-operation, the United States has provided Kyrgyzstan with various forms of assistance worth about $2 billion. In order to strengthen democracy and ensure the transparency and legitimacy of electoral processes, the

United States has allocated significant funds to Kyrgyzstan. For example, from 2010 to 2016, the U.S. grant aid totalled more than \$17 million. Kyrgyzstan has undergone a great number of democratic and liberal reforms at the U.S.'s encouragement, and according to former U.S. Ambassador to the Kyrgyz Republic Pamela Spratlen, "Kyrgyzstan is the only emerging democracy in Central Asia.[16]

A new stage of Kyrgyz-American relations began on 10 July 2014, when the US military base was completely withdrawn from the territory of Kyrgyzstan and Kyrgyzstan's foreign policy turned towards Russia. In 2015, at the initiative of the Kyrgyz side, the cooperation agreement of 1993, under which Kyrgyzstan received humanitarian, economic and technical assistance, was cancelled. At the same time, all supplies within the framework of assistance and cooperation programmes were not subject to tax and customs payments.

With the withdrawal of the military base and denunciation of the agreement, the U.S. lost its political leverage, but began to actively strengthen its position in civil society. Kyrgyzstan is currently the only Central Asian state where US political technologists have a large number of tools to implement their strategies. On the territory of the Kyrgyz Republic, the United States has created a huge network of non-governmental organisations, media, educational institutions and groups in social networks involved in the manipulation of public consciousness. The United States allocates grants for the implementation of projects, which, as a rule, are aimed at discrediting the current government and shaping anti-Russian sentiments. There is no doubt that the United States does not plan to curtail relations with Kyrgyzstan. This is indirectly confirmed by the construction of the new building of the US Embassy and the new campus of the American University.

At this stage, U.S. interests in Kyrgyzstan are pursued within the framework of the Greater Central Asia project formulated in 2005 and aimed at "democratising" the region, removing Central Asian states from Russian geopolitical influence and uniting them into a single region with Afghanistan. The withdrawal of Central Asia from Russia's influence is necessary for the United States, as it will strengthen Russia's international and economic isolation, complicate communications between Russia and Iran, and weaken Russia's control over the threats of terrorism and drug trafficking on its southern borders. In addition, the format of relations between Kyrgyzstan and the U.S. at this stage directly depends on relations

---

[16] US ambassador: Kyrgyzstan is the only developing democracy in CA *AND* http://www.vb.kg/doc/279480 posol ssha: kyrgyzstan edinstvennaia razvivaushaiasia demokratiia v ca.h tail

between the Kyrgyz Republic and the Russian Federation.

In addition, Kyrgyzstan and the United States have started co-operation within the framework of the ambitious New Silk Road project, which involves the development of infrastructure and trade and economic ties between Central and South Asian states, as well as CASA-1000, which involves the transit of electricity from Kyrgyzstan and Tajikistan to Afghanistan and Pakistan. These projects are aimed at the independent socio-economic development of Afghanistan after the withdrawal of the US military contingent from there.[17]

In addition, the largest drug trafficking from Afghanistan to Russia passes through the territory of Central Asia and Kyrgyzstan in particular. It is noteworthy that the U.S. only imitates the fight against the drug problem, while not allowing the eradication of opium poppy crops on the territory of Afghanistan. For comparison, the main drug traffic to the US territory comes from Colombia, where the US is reducing coca bush crops in every possible way. The main market for Afghan narcotics is Russia, whose undermining of democratic potential plays into the hands of the United States. The U.S. promotes the expansion of transport infrastructure between Afghanistan and Central Asian states, supports the reduction of barriers on the borders of Central Asia and Afghanistan, and financially and informationally supports the withdrawal of Russian border troops from the southern borders of Kyrgyzstan and Tajikistan. Moreover, the U.S. actively co-operates with Kyrgyzstan's anti-drug structures, participated in their creation and continues to actively co-operate with them.

Cooperation with Kyrgyzstan enables the US not to leave Central Asia, which is a convenient springboard for controlling the situation in China, Russia, oil fields in Iraq, containing Iran, etc. Close cooperation between the Kyrgyz Republic and the U.S. in the field of security and defence continues, which is expressed in a number of activities, such as training of Kyrgyz military and law enforcement officers in U.S. educational centres or joint anti-terrorist exercises. In addition, the U.S. supports pro-Western politicians by financing their trips and organising various events for them.

In addition, the U.S. suggests that the model of developing relations with Kyrgyzstan could serve as a model for building relations with other states in the region. U.S. administration officials have repeatedly stated that Kyrgyzstan's experience in building

---

[17] See: *Umarov A.A.* Strategic Initiatives of the United States and China in Central Asia *and* Comparative Politics.-2015.- No. 1 (18).-S. 131.

parliamentary democracy is unique and of great value to Central Asian states.[18]

At the same time, it should be noted that the United States does not care about stability in Kyrgyzstan and Central Asia as a whole. Moreover, the situation of chaos plays into their hands, as it destabilises the situation on the borders of Russia and China, weakening them. For this purpose, the United States has repeatedly provoked conflicts and contradictions within Kyrgyz society, shaking up the situation.

Russia, on the contrary, is interested in stability in Kyrgyzstan and in strengthening its position in the region. To this end, Russia is ready to pour large investments into the real sectors of the Kyrgyz economy, unlike the United States, which allocates funds for democratisation projects that do not have any constructive component. Since Kyrgyzstan's accession to the EAEU, Russia's investment projects have increased: the acquisition of Kyrgyzgaz by Gazprom and the construction of the Kambar-Ata HPP cascade. The bulk of Russian investment is in the energy sector (76%[19]), most of which is allocated by Gazprom as part of an investment programme providing for gasification of certain regions of the country, construction of the North-South pipeline aimed at gasification of the southern regions, reconstruction of the gas transmission network and exploration work. In the future, Kyrgyzstan may act as an energy and transport corridor to Pakistan, India and China.

In addition, Kyrgyzstan is a buffer zone between the Russian Federation and Afghanistan, which is a source of drug crime and terrorism and poses a threat to Russian security. Military and political co-operation with Kyrgyzstan, therefore, is in many ways a guarantee of security of the Russian borders, and explains the presence of five Russian military facilities on the territory of the republic. Also, the Russian Federation takes part in personnel training for the armed forces of the republic, conducts joint military and anti-terrorist exercises, provides military-technical assistance to the security structures of the Kyrgyz Republic, and cooperates with the Kyrgyz Republic in the field of air defence. Since joining the EAEU, the volume of direct Russian military-technical assistance totalled $1.1 billion.

Russia's position is attractive for Kyrgyzstan because, unlike the United States, it does not insist on democratisation and does not seek to introduce its own experience. In addition,

---

[18] See: US Strategic Interests in Central Asia // http://polit- asia.kz/index.php/analytics/arkhiv-materialovpi/2015/758-strategicheskie-mteresy-ssha-v-tsentralnoj-azii
[19] See: *Margulis S.* Kyrgyzstan's accession to the EAEU and Russia's interests. - M., 2016. - C. 14.

the Russian Federation does not interact with opposition representatives to participate in domestic political processes and does not participate in domestic politics under the guise of human rights or other similar activities.

Russia's main goal is to prevent Kyrgyzstan from falling out from under its geopolitical influence, to preserve the cultural and civilisational unity of the states, and to maintain a state of stability and security. In addition, Russia seeks to prevent the United States from gaining a foothold in Kyrgyzstan by maintaining a loyal political regime and politicians. However, the difficulty here is that the fragmentation of Kyrgyzstan's political elite limits the possibility of effective interaction with it on the part of the Russian Federation. In addition, there is a growing nationalist sentiment in Kyrgyz society, the carriers of which have a generally negative attitude towards the Russian Federation and deny Russia's cultural and historical contribution to the development of Kyrgyz society.

In general, Russia's main strategic interest in Kyrgyzstan is to consolidate its position in Central Asia and prevent the region from slipping out of its control, as it is vital for Russia to maintain its status as a Eurasian power.

At the same time, Russia seeks to maintain partnership relations with another Central Asian geopolitical player - China. In May 2015, the heads of Russia and China signed a joint co-operation agreement between the EAEU and China's Silk Road Economic Belt project. The pairing of these two projects has excellent prospects, as it offers the ability to successfully complement each other due to the fact that the projects are not mutually exclusive (the EAEU is an integration project, while the EGPTTP is an infrastructure and transport project).

China, unlike the previous actors in Kyrgyzstan, has mainly economic interests, although it is also interested in the stability and security of its western borders.

China is the largest investor in the Kyrgyz economy. Kyrgyzstan is China's third largest trading partner in the CIS countries after the Russian Federation and the Republic of Kazakhstan. Over the years of cooperation between Kyrgyzstan and China, more than 10 state investment agreements have been signed for a total amount of almost $1.9 billion, which does not include grant funding. At the initial stage, China provided large commodity loans, as well as loans for the construction of a joint venture to produce paper. In addition, China has financed the rehabilitation of road infrastructure: the construction of the Osh-Sary-Tash-Ishketam road was completed in 2012, and the Bishkek-Naryn-Torugart motorway is currently under reconstruction. In addition, new agreements on road reconstruction have been signed between Kyrgyzstan and China, the financing of which is approximately $130 million.[20]

At the current stage, 74% of direct investment from the Chinese side is directed to the energy, gas and geological exploration sectors. At the same time, investments are directed to those areas that are not oriented towards the markets of the EAEU states. Conversely, Chinese investments in industry and processing, whose products are exported to the Russian Federation and the Republic of Kazakhstan, have significantly decreased since Kyrgyzstan joined the EAEU. It is interesting to note that Chinese investments, as a rule, are allocated on the condition of mandatory purchase of Chinese machinery and equipment, i.e. they support Chinese industry. During the state visit of the Prime Minister of the Kyrgyz Republic to China in December 2015, three main areas of cooperation were highlighted: the construction of a ring road around Issyk-Kul, the construction of the China-Kyrgyzstan railway, and the relocation of a number of manufacturing enterprises from China to the territory of Kyrgyzstan.

The most promising vector of cooperation between Kyrgyzstan and China is the concept of "One Belt, One Road" - a project that covers a significant part of Eurasia, uniting developing and developed countries on the basis of strengthening bilateral and multilateral cooperation with the participation of China. As applied to Kyrgyzstan, this project is being implemented in the following areas:

- reconstruction of roads and railways to transport goods from China to the Middle East, the Caucasus and Europe.

- construction of new roads, railways, pipelines, transport and logistics infrastructure;

- transit of energy resources to China (gas from Uzbekistan and Turkmenistan);

- establishment of Chinese enterprises in Kyrgyzstan for the local market, as well as for the export of final products to China and the EAEU states;

- investments from China in the KR economy;

- co-operation on the border of China and Kyrgyzstan, formation of a free trade zone.

In addition, since the early 2000s, China has been trying to implement a railway project that could link the XUAR capital Kashgar and Uzbek Andijan, as there are currently only two railway lines in XUAR that lead to Kazakhstan. The China-Kyrgyzstan-Uzbekistan railway

---

[20] See: *Baktygulov Sh.* China and Kyrgyzstan: Main Challenges and Trends of Cooperation // http://cabar.asia/ru/sheradil-baktygulov-kitaj-i-kyrgyzstan-osnovnye-vyzovy-i-tendentsii-sotrudnichestva/

project, which has been under discussion for the past decade, could become the largest bilateral project, with an estimated cost of $6.5 billion. The project has already received support at the level of the heads of republics, but opinions differ on the feasibility of the project: some insist on its rapid implementation, while others fear potential Chinese expansion. The construction of the China-Kyrgyzstan-Uzbekistan railway will open access not only to the Central Asian states, but also to Iran and Pakistan. The difficulties of the project's implementation are that China and Kyrgyzstan have not reached a compromise on the route of the railway. It is favourable for China to lay the railway with a short length of about 100 km. The Kyrgyz side insists that the railway should cover as many settlements as possible and offers two options for laying the railway - 433 and 278 km long.[21]

In general, China's interests in the Kyrgyz Republic can be conditionally divided into 3 groups:

1) Geopolitical. By extending influence in Kyrgyzstan and maintaining border security, China seeks to ensure development and security in its western provinces, particularly in Xinjiang.

2) Energy. Due to the fact that China aims to diversify energy corridors and resource suppliers, Kyrgyzstan is able to provide China with conditions for safe transit of hydrocarbons. To date, about 80% of oil supplies to China are realised through the Strait of Malacca, which is controlled by the US Navy, thus creating a certain dependence of the Chinese energy system on them. Construction of land transport corridors through the territory of Kyrgyzstan will make it possible to remove oil transit from the influence of the USA.

3) Economic. Kyrgyzstan is the main trading partner of China's western provinces. Over 80 per cent of trade turnover between China and Central Asia is in XUAR, which borders Kyrgyzstan.

In addition, Kyrgyzstan is able to provide a transport corridor for Chinese goods, which can provide PRC access to the markets of Iran and Europe.

Thus, Kyrgyzstan has voluntarily or involuntarily become an object of political strategies of three world powers - Russia, the United States and China. And if the interests of Russia and China are more or less on the same plane: ensuring effective development of the state, stable economic growth, maintenance of security and order on the territory of the

---

[21] See: *Panfilova V.* Chinese financial noose tightens on Bishkek/ http://www.ng.ru/cis/2017- 05-15/6 6988 kirgisia.htinl

republic (despite the different goals: for Russia - consolidation of its geopolitical influence, for China - economic and energy security of the western provinces), the United States of America is trying not to lose its geopolitical influence in the region, ousting Russia from there, while using the whole arsenal of available methods, up to provocation The political leadership of the country tried to realise a rather successful idea - balancing the competing interests of geopolitical players, which can provide opportunities for political bargaining. In practice, however, it turned out that Kyrgyzstan could not cope with such a task: manoeuvring between the three players led to inconsistency in its foreign policy course, lack of understanding of its national interests and priorities, and constant search for economic preferences to the detriment of political strategies.

CHAPTER 3

PROBLEMATIC SEGMENTS OF THE POLITICAL SYSTEM OF THE KYRGYZ REPUBLIC IN THE CONTEXT OF EXTERNAL INFLUENCE

The political system of the Kyrgyz Republic, since the collapse of the USSR and up to the present day, is at the stage of its formation and formation as a democratic, social and legal system, as stated in the Constitution of the Kyrgyz Republic. Such a system is referred to as transitional or transitory, i.e. in the process of transition from Soviet totalitarianism to modern democracy. It is important to note that for Kyrgyzstan this period of transformation of the political system has been prolonged, as traditional institutions together with the Soviet legacy have a strong influence in the state. Consequently, in the political system of Kyrgyzstan, even in a democracy, there will always be some elements of traditionality and the Soviet past.

A significant feature of the political system of Kyrgyzstan is that its formation and the formation of its institutions have always taken place under the influence of a third interested state. The reason for this lies in the fact that after the collapse of the Soviet Union, subsidies to the republic from the Centre ceased and the newly independent state had to form its political system in the absence of the necessary resources. This situation was skilfully exploited by the United States of America, which was among the first to establish diplomatic relations with Kyrgyzstan and began to actively participate in the formation of a situation within the country that would be favourable to the United States itself.

At the behest of the United States of America, Kyrgyzstan became the first Central Asian state in which opposition to the ruling Communist Party began to form and which embarked on the path of democratisation. It is no secret that one of the goals of United States foreign policy is the widespread imposition of liberal democracy. Having recognised the universality of liberal values, the US administration is trying to oblige almost every state in the world to follow them. The desire to democratise the political system and reform the economy along the lines of the liberal model led to the fact that the vector of Kyrgyzstan's development became oriented towards Western countries and the United States, which in every possible way sought to expand the sphere of interaction with Kyrgyzstan. The United States provided various kinds of assistance to the newly independent state: financial and institutional assistance, organised educational programmes for the population of the Kyrgyz Republic, and actively promoted Kyrgyzstan's participation in various international financial

20

institutions controlled by the American government, which began to actively credit the economy of developing Kyrgyzstan.

However, such liberalisation and modernisation of the political system towards democracy turned out for the Kyrgyz Republic with the signing of the Washington Consensus, a programme that was initially formulated for Latin American states that were in debt dependence on financial institutions. The main goal of this programme was to create such a situation within these states that would ensure the repayment of loans to American financial institutions. For the Kyrgyz Republic the result of this act was the assumption of obligations to reduce social expenditures, expenditures on mass consumption goods, food products, increase the income tax rate, increase lending rates while reducing the volume of loans, open the borders to imports of goods, ensure a free exchange rate of the national currency, widespread privatisation and transfer of industry from state financing to credit.[22]

In 1993, cooperation between Kyrgyzstan and the International Monetary Fund began, but the blind transfer of market models of economy to the economic system of Kyrgyzstan without taking into account the objective peculiarities of the Kyrgyz reality did not modernise the system, but led to the actual destruction of the real sector of the economy. The decline in industrial production over the next two years was approximately 78%, the volume of state-owned enterprises decreased from 45.4% to 3.4%, which was not without the participation of international financial institutions that insisted on privatisation of state-owned enterprises. In addition, the World Bank in 1998 issued a loan to restructure unprofitable industrial facilities, which led to their bankruptcy.[23]

At the behest of the same Western monetary institutions, Kyrgyzstan, the first among the CIS states, joined the WTO in 1998, as a result of which the remnants of industrial enterprises in the country finally ceased to function. The catastrophic economic situation in the country almost led Kyrgyzstan in 2006 to join the Heavily Indebted Poor Countries (HIPC) programme, a group of the world's poorest countries with high levels of financial indebtedness. This programme provides for the cancellation of part of the debt on condition that economic reforms are implemented under the strict control of the World Bank and the International Monetary Fund, which would have put the country on a par with the poorest

---

[22] See: *Ivanov S.G. The* role of foreign policy factors in the processes of transformation of the economy of the Kyrgyz Republic. - Б., 2009. - C. 219.
[23] See: *Knyazev A.A.* Vectors and paradigms of Kyrgyz independence (Essays on post-Soviet history). -B., 2012.-P. 60.

African states and led to the loss of the ability to independently pursue economic policy.

Preferential lending by Western monetary institutions to the Kyrgyz economy under the condition of its liberalisation, although to some extent replacing Soviet subsidies, allowing the state to fulfil its social obligations to the population, ultimately led to Kyrgyzstan's dependence on the opinion of Western states in formulating its political course, as most of the Kyrgyz state debt is owed to US-controlled financial institutions, such as the World Bank, the Asian Development Bank and the International Monetary Fund.

Kyrgyzstan's political system, as well as its economic system, has become hostage to the strategic interests of the United States. Democratisation of political institutions and active cooperation with the US have not made Kyrgyzstan an equal participant in the world community. "The Kyrgyz Republic has joined the ranks of "grey zone" countries: semi-democracy, formal democracy, electoral democracy, illiberal democracy, facade democracy, virtual democracy, pseudo-democracy, which are characterised by a state of permanent social tension fraught with periodic aggravations in the form of mass protests and illegitimate change of power".[24]

At the same time, the reforming of the most important institutions of the political system also took place under the permanent influence of the United States on this process. Thus, in 2005, on the eve of the coup d'état, the United States allocated over $2.5 million to support democracy in the Kyrgyz Republic.[25] This money was used to purchase equipment for marking voters, to train independent observers, to train the staff of local election commissions, and to implement NGO and media projects related to the electoral process. In addition, the US actively participated in the adoption of the new Election Code, providing both financial and advisory assistance, and contributed to the technical modernisation of the Central Election Commission of the Kyrgyz Republic. Undoubtedly, under such conditions, it is a stretch to speak about the independence of the CEC and the electoral process in the Kyrgyz Republic from external influence. In addition, the USA actively forced the reform of legislation in terms of protection of human rights, freedom of religion, equality of ethnic minorities, freedom of speech and mass media, which allowed them to impose Western models of behaviour and norms of morality and ethics on society.

---

[24] *Muratalieva 3.* Foreign policy of Kyrgyzstan in the period of independence // http://www.mirperemen. net/content/ vneshnyaya-politika-kyrgyzstana-perioda-nezavisimosti (24 May 2016)

[25] See: *Kazakpaev M.* USA-Kyrgyzstan: a model of interaction of non-equilibrium participants / Central Asia and Caucasus. - 2006. - № 3(45). - C. 61.

The security sector of the Kyrgyz Republic is also being reformed at the behest and at the expense of the United States. Active cooperation between the United States and Kyrgyzstan in the area of security and defence began after September 11, 2001, and for many years now the U.S. State Department has been allocating significant financial resources to reform the Ministry of Defence, anti-terrorist, anti-drug and other special services, and to train personnel. The implementation of such projects, firstly, allows Americans to thoroughly study the structure and composition of government agencies responsible for security, as well as to freely receive information about the current situation in the country and the region as a whole. Secondly, such projects create conditions for ensuring loyalty to the West on the part of employees of the security agencies of the Kyrgyz Republic. For example, in 2005, I. Isakov, whose son was serving as a liaison officer at the headquarters of the US Central Command, was appointed Minister of Defence.[26]

Another feature of the political system of the Kyrgyz Republic is a well-developed civil society. The number of registered non-governmental organisations is several times higher than that of its Central Asian neighbours and exceeds 16,000. NGOs are actively involved in all spheres of Kyrgyz society, defending the implementation of citizens' rights and freedoms, monitoring the electoral process, engaging in research activities, and so on. However, this sphere is not without the active participation of the United States. The United States provides significant funding to the non-governmental sector, taking advantage of the fact that external funding of public associations in the Kyrgyz Republic is not restricted or monitored at the state level. Thus, non-governmental organisations financed by the West, led by the United States, implement projects often aimed not at solving internal problems of Kyrgyz society, but at promoting the interests of Western states: ensuring transparency of the electoral process, liberalisation of the economy and political system, reforming the judicial system, public administration, etc., thus ensuring control over the main political processes in the state.

It is non-governmental organisations that become the instrument through which the United States brings the right politicians to power in the KR and influences the adoption of important political decisions, which allows it to implement its own strategic plans. In order to be able to use all levers of influence on internal processes in the state, the United States

---

[26] See: Ruslan Isakov: "Consideration of my father's case is the height of hypocrisy and cynicism" // http://www.fergananews. com/articles/6438

implements its main task - to prevent centralisation of power, as well as monopolisation of power in one hand. Thus, the first President of the Republic, Akaev, concentrated all power mechanisms in his hands. He could independently form the Government, determine its structure, appoint and dismiss the heads of ministries, local judges, as well as the heads of LSG bodies. The President single-handedly controlled all the leading sectors of the economy, creating various state bodies for this purpose without including them in the Government, and directed them through the Presidential Administration.[27] It was precisely this state of affairs that displeased the United States administration and limited the opportunities for their participation. The result was that, through a large number of non-governmental organisations, the US organised a coup d'état, skilfully exploiting social tensions and channelling this destructive energy in the direction they wanted.

However, the ultimate goal of the United States was not a formal change of leadership, but the formation of a political system in which U.S. participation in domestic processes would be maximised. This political system was to be a system with a parliamentary form of government combined with a developed civil sector.

The point here is that such a political system - parliamentarism combined with a strong civil society - is very vulnerable to outside interference. In such a system, power is horizontal rather than vertical, divided into branches, decentralised and distributed among independent groups and individuals, which enables the US to influence political, economic and other strategic decision-making through its agents.

In addition, under parliamentarism, the property hierarchy is often transformed into a power hierarchy, since it is not individual competent and strong-willed individuals who come to power, but individuals with financial capital who are able to "buy" a place on the party list for a certain amount of money. It is no secret that the true purpose of such aspirations to power is not the desire to serve for the good of the state, but rather the prospect of multiplying personal capital. Of course, it is quite easy to get the opinion of such a parliamentarian in exchange for a fixed fee.

In addition, the parliamentary form of government is also convenient for external influence because even if persons who are clearly aware of and protect the state interests come

---

[27] See: Constitutional Reform in the Kyrgyz Republic: Achievements and Problems. Report by O. Tekebaev at the international conference "The Impact of Constitutional Processes in Post-Communist Transformation", 3-4 November 2014, Yerevan, Armenia *And* http://kabarlar.org/news/34498-konstitucionnaya-reforma-v-kyrgyzskoy-respublike-dostizheniya-i- problemy.html

to power, it is not difficult to provoke a political crisis under such a system and dissolve the country's leadership altogether, since the absence of a strong centralised authority makes it possible to plunge the state into chaos by stirring up contradictions between various religious, ethnic and political groups, which exist in any society in one way or another.[28]

However, Kurmanbek Bakiyev, who succeeded Askar Akayev as president, did not fulfil the expectations of the United States and was in no hurry to reform the political system towards parliamentarianism. The United States responded by organising opposition demonstrations, which were held for almost a year, demanding constitutional reform, the resignation of the president and the formation of a coalition government. In November 2006, Bakiyev relented and began to reform the Constitution. However, the result was the adoption of the Constitution in 2007, which formally proclaimed a parliamentary form of government, but in fact all the main power institutions remained under the control of the President. Undoubtedly, the West was not satisfied with this scenario, which was reflected in the negative opinion of the Venice Commission on the adopted version of the Constitution, in which the experts noted the tendency to authoritarianism, violation of the principle of separation of powers, etc.[29] Consequently, the reform of the political system remained only a matter of time.

The constitutional reform of 2010, which proclaimed parliamentarism in the republic, satisfied the West, led by the USA, which was already reflected in the positive conclusion of the Venice Commission, according to which the Constitution fully complies with all democratic standards.[30] The establishment of parliamentarism in the republic was also facilitated by the fact that one of the features of the political system of the Kyrgyz Republic is multipartyism. The number of political parties in the country at the beginning of 2017, according to the Ministry of Justice, reached 223.[31] In Kyrgyzstan, there are both popular parties and parties that are completely unknown to the majority of the population, uniting fellow countrymen, colleagues, fellow villagers, relatives, etc. around the leader.

Thus, the formation in Kyrgyzstan of a political system with a parliamentary form of

---

[28] See: *Erkimbaev B.* Kyrgyzstan. Constitutional reform: "fool-proofing" or still geopolitics? // http://www.centrasia.ru/newsA.php?st=1452840900

[29] Opinion on the Constitutional situation in the Kyrgyz Republic adopted by the Commission at its 73rd Plenary Session (Venice, 14-15 December 2007) // http://www.venice.coe.int/webforms/documents/?pdf=CDL-AD(2007)045-e

[30] See: Conclusion on the Draft Constitution of the Kyrgyz Republic (version published on 21 May 2010). Adopted by the Venice Commission at its 83rd plenary session (Venice, 4 June 2010) // http://www.venice.coe.int/webforms/documents/?pdf=CDL-AD(2010)015-rus

[31] See: List of political parties // http://miniust.gov.kg/7page_id=6551

government and a developed civil society can well be called a success of the United States policy. In general, by 2010 the situation was such that almost all power institutions, agencies and even regions of the state were in one way or another included in the process of active co-operation with the United States.

The changes began around 2010, when Kyrgyzstan's policy began to gradually turn towards the Russian Federation and CIS colleagues, distancing itself from the United States. As a result, in 2014, at the initiative of the Kyrgyz side, the NATO military base, which had been based on the territory of the Kyrgyz Republic for about 13 years, ceased to function. The next step was the denunciation of the agreement between the Kyrgyz Republic and the United States in July 2015, under which, since 1993, Kyrgyzstan had received significant assistance from the U.S. Government, including financial assistance: "The denunciation of the Agreement as of 20 August 2015 will affect all areas of cooperation between the parties, covering activities and projects implemented under the international treaty in question, including USAID projects. This will be expressed in the termination of tax and customs privileges, cancellation of privileges and immunities for US citizens (involved in projects), equivalent to administrative and technical personnel, etc. And in general, denunciation will affect all persons involved in the implementation of projects based on the denounced Agreement".[32] The reason for the unilateral termination of the agreement was the awarding by the U.S. government of the "Human Rights Defender" award to A. Askarov, a citizen of the Kyrgyz Republic, who was convicted in his home country of Kyrgyzstan for organising the ethnic conflict in the south of the republic in 2010, during which a large number of people died, in particular for inciting ethnic hatred, participation in hostage-taking, killing of law enforcement officers, etc. The reason for the cooling of US relations is most likely due to the realisation of the priority of developing relations with Russia and joining the Eurasian Economic Union and the Customs Union. In addition to the geographical, historical and civilizational proximity of the Kyrgyz Republic and the Russian Federation, one of the factors behind the Kyrgyz Republic's accession to the Eurasian integration associations was the threat of introducing a visa regime for migrant workers from countries outside the union to enter Russia. Such a situation could have catastrophic consequences for Kyrgyzstan - increased unemployment, a sharp drop in living standards, and, as a consequence, popular uprisings:

---

[32] Kyrgyzstan-US relations are undergoing a serious transformation *And* http://www.stanradar.com/news/full/ 18108-otnoshenija-kyrgyzstana-i-ssha-perezhivajut-sereznuju- transformatsiju.html (25 May 2016)

remittances from migrant workers account for 33% of the republic's GDP.[33]

In general, analysing the political system of the Kyrgyz Republic, we can conclude that it was formed in a state of constant dependence on the interests of external states and, in particular, the United States. The reason for this lies in the inability of the state to fulfil its obligations on its own without external financial assistance, which made the republic hostage to the strategic interests of its donors. The result of this state of affairs is that the modern political system of the Kyrgyz Republic is unable to fulfil its main functions, such as ensuring the stability of political power, its legitimisation, effective management of various spheres of life of the state's population, timely response to the interests and demands of society, its integration, and, in general, everything that ensures the safety and stability of the system, as it is constantly dependent on external influence. Overcoming such impact in the future may well become a guarantee of effective development of a stable political system of Kyrgyzstan, but for this purpose it is necessary to choose such a strategic partner, which will be interested in the realisation of its own interests, first of all, through overcoming the state of chaos and ensuring stability in the Kyrgyz Republic. Such a partner for Kyrgyzstan may well be the Russian Federation, which is no less interested than Kyrgyzstan itself in establishing a strong government and maintaining stability in the state. This is conditioned not only by the fact that Kyrgyzstan is a buffer zone between the borders of the Russian Federation and unstable Afghanistan, but also by the fact that a large number of Russian citizens live on the territory of the Kyrgyz Republic and it is the direct responsibility of the Russian Federation to ensure their security.

---

[33] See: Experts of the Moscow Carnegie Centre on the 25th anniversary of independence of the Kyrgyz Republic // http://zanoza.kg/doc/343655_eksperty_moskovskogo_centra_kamegi_on_25_letii_nezavisimosti_kr.html

CHAPTER 4

WAYS OF COUNTERACTING EXTERNAL INFLUENCE ON THE INTERNAL POLITICAL PROCESS (ON THE EXAMPLE OF THE KYRGYZ REPUBLIC)

In the context of permanent external influence on the internal processes of independent states by third countries, the implementation of countermeasures is particularly relevant. The modern reality is that the United States, implementing its strategic geopolitical plans, shamelessly interferes in the internal politics of other states, bringing to power convenient political regimes, imposing liberal values, destroying traditional historical and cultural ties, artificially pushing ethnicisation and regionalisation, etc. The state of permanent chaos inside the state that is the object of influence plays into the hands of the United States, as it allows it to consolidate its influence in this state, and thus, if not to influence its geopolitical rivals, then to be located in close proximity to their borders.

Such a problem has not bypassed the Kyrgyz Republic, where internal political processes for a long time have not been without attention and active participation of the US administration. The difficulty lies in the fact that the political leadership of the country does not seek to defend the sovereignty of its state and does not take any real actions to ensure the security of the country's political system from external influences. The goals of ensuring internal security of the Kyrgyz Republic are declared in such normative acts as the Concept of National Security of the Kyrgyz Republic approved by the Decree of the President of the Kyrgyz Republic dated 9 June 2012 and the National Strategy for Sustainable Development of the Kyrgyz Republic for the period 2013-2017. These programme foreign policy documents enshrine the need to ensure internal state security, information security, security of the political system, and even contain a provision on the formatting of public attitudes and processes in the interests of security and development of the Republic. However, in reality, these documents in terms of ensuring the protection of the political system from external influence remain only programme acts without any real political actions. In addition, neither the Concept nor the Strategy are legal acts of direct action (the Concept is a system of ideas, on the basis of which other normative acts are adopted in the future, which should not contradict it, and the Development Strategy is a set of plans and tasks to be implemented in the specified period). Accordingly, neither document implies institutional control over their implementation.

In view of the above, it can be stated that at this stage of Kyrgyzstan's development, mechanisms to counter external influence are either absent or do not meet the current realities, or do not have practical implementation. Consequently, it is necessary to develop real practical steps to neutralise the impact of third countries, using: a) positive experience of foreign partners, b) mechanisms and strategies proposed by experts, and c) own internal resources.

In the world practice there are the following strategies to counteract the mechanisms of external influence, soft power and network technologies:

1)   The strategy of vigilance consists in vigilance against possible internal and external latent and explicit threats by informing the population about the latest political and psychological mechanisms for manipulating consciousness, undermining statehood, and destroying the cultural and religious foundations of society.

2)   The strategy of sustainability consists in the formation of such state, social institutions and mass consciousness that will be able to resist attempts of external and internal destabilisation of the political and social systems of society.

3)   The strategy of countering network technologies of undermining statehood consists in the widespread dissemination in the media of reliable information about the current state of affairs in the state and defending one's own interpretation of world events.

4)   The strategy of maintaining social optimism is to establish a high level of support for the state apparatus and law enforcement agencies among the population through the introduction of a national idea, the formation of ideology, especially against the background of a successful policy of the state in the field of defence of state interests and national security.[34]

A. Manoilo, a Russian researcher, Doctor of Political Science, suggested the following ways of countering external influence:

1)   Use mechanisms and technologies of the same level, as separate measures, methods and means will be fruitless.

2)   Timely identify the channels of money for the implementation of "colour

---

[34] See: *V.V. Karyakin*. Russia as a target of realisation of strategies of "indirect actions" and "soft power" of foreign policy authors. Report at the scientific and practical conference "Strategic management in the sphere of national security of Russia: subjects, resources, technologies"// https://riss.ru/analitycs/2695/

revolutions" and promptly stop their functioning. Here the logic is simple: no funds for the revolution - no revolution. At the same time, it should be taken into account that the infusion of money into the recipient state of "colour revolutions" strategies starts one and a half to two years before the proposed event.

It is noteworthy that in the Kyrgyz Republic receipts of funds to the accounts of NGOs are not tracked in any way at all: there is no need to agree on the receipt of foreign funding, there is no procedure for registering these funds with state authorities, and there are no special reporting requirements. Moreover, foreign funding is not singled out as a special unit of income and is equated with domestic funding.

3)   Ideologise young people between the ages of 16 and 35, as this social group is the main strike force of disobedience actions, it is young people who have become the social basis of all "colour revolutions".

Overcoming the ideological mobility of youth, involving young people in patriotically oriented public associations, and popularising sports will make it possible to avoid external manipulation of this part of the population and using it as a resource for a coup d'état.

In the conditions of the Kyrgyz Republic, it is necessary to pay attention to the unemployment among young people, the lack of mechanisms for socialisation and self-realisation, the low percentage of education and demographic growth, which contributes to the fact that the young population is members of extremist organisations, easily manipulated and is an absolutely manageable resource for the implementation of various actions, sometimes even disadvantageous to them.

4)   Pay attention to regional problems. A. Manoilo focuses special attention on the North Caucasus, Siberia and the Far Eastern region of Russia, as the organisers of the "colour revolution" can take as an ideological basis the slogans of separatism under the leadership of regional leaders.[35]

In the Kyrgyz Republic, it is necessary to pay attention to the problems of regionalism and ethnic equality. Since the south of the republic, the Fergana Valley, has the highest population density, population growth, and unemployment rate, the south of Kyrgyzstan is densely populated by ethnic Uzbeks, who are neighbours of the Kyrgyz, while differing mentally and culturally. Artificially manipulated ethnicisation has repeatedly led to bloody

---

[35] See: *Mikryukov V.* A remedy for unobtrusive aggression // http://vpk-news.ru/articles/29342

ethnic conflicts.

In general, it is possible to resist the strategies of external influence through modernisation of the political system of the state, implementation of a number of reforms in the field of social security, education in order to stabilise the regime by introducing to the population the idea of systemic development of the state, movement on the path of progress, and, first of all, through a competent information policy. Thus, when confronting soft power mechanisms, the task of the state lies, first of all, in ensuring the protection of information, cultural, civilisational and value and attitudinal spheres, as "soft power" technologies, external influence, network technologies mostly harm public interests and values, and only then the stability of the political system.

The objects of such protection will be the information environment and information resources, the system of formation of public opinion and consciousness, the system of political decision-making at any level, the psyche and behaviour of the population. The tools for ensuring such security are the media, the Internet, non-governmental organisations and humanitarian-information means. These institutions are able to unite society around a single national idea, are the transmitters of historical memory, spiritual values and national culture.[36]

Researchers agree that the mental state of the population, political moods of the masses are of great importance for the stability of the political system. Consequently, the primary task is to ensure a comfortable psychological state of the population through the creation of a multilevel system for ensuring psychological security.

Thus, in order to establish external influence on internal processes in the state, first of all, it is necessary to take control of the information sphere, through which it is possible to attract politically active part of the population of the republic. Hence, it is necessary not only to control the media, the Internet and other information resources, but also to implement, through the above-mentioned resources, state strategies aimed at attracting supporters, increasing their political potential, and establishing a positive image of the authorities. In addition, it is necessary to provide the population with an attractive idea based on traditional values, which can compete with the liberal ideas of the West. Such an idea should be actively

---

[36] See: *Sinchuk Y.V., Sinchuk I.Yu.* To the question of strengthening the national security of the state in the context of "soft power" / The role of "soft power" technologies in information, value and attitudinal and civilizational confrontation / Academy of Military Sciences, Scientific Research Centre for National Security Problems, Department of Information Analytics and Political Technologies of Bauman Moscow State Technical University / Edited by I.V. Bocharnikov. - M, 2016. - C.246.

broadcast in the media, social networks, popular bloggers and public figures. At the same time, such an idea should be carefully conceptualised in order to attract all segments of society, from the general public to the intellectual elite.

In addition, it is interesting to note the opinion of researchers that in order to successfully counteract external influence, the state must have a strong enough patriotic opposition, which will attract to its ranks a politically active population on various issues that disagree with the official policy of the authorities. Such an entity should represent the protesting part of the population of the state, but at the same time be independent from the influence of third states. The leadership of this opposition group (party, faction or association) should have sufficient intellectual potential and high awareness in order to respond to the protest moods in a timely manner, attracting the people and being able to lead the protest masses in order to prevent the loss of control over the protesters. Of course, such an opposition should be supported in every possible way by the official authorities by providing it with funding, access to information resources, benefits and other privileges, so that such an organisation does not need to seek allies among Western institutions. In this case, there will be a real opposition mechanism in the state, capable of expressing the will of the protesting part of the population, but at the same time it will be patriotic and partly controlled by the current government.[37]

In addition, one should take into account the fact that any external influence on internal processes in the state is based, first of all, on the globalisation of the political and financial elite, which entails the weakness of the state's sovereignty. That is, if representatives of the government and big business are not financially or otherwise bound to Western countries, do not have real estate in Europe or America, do not have accounts in Western banks, do not receive education at the expense of Western funds, the possibility of implementing Western intervention technologies in the state is reduced to a minimum.

In general, taking into account the considered opinion of researchers, we can come to the conclusion that in the conditions of Central Asia and the Kyrgyz Republic in particular, the ways of countering technologies of external influence should be based on two types of resources.

Speaking about internal resources, we should start from the fact that the ultimate goal

---

[37] See: *Sivkov K.* Complex Counteraction // http://ru-an.mfo/news/2557/

of establishing external influence in the state, in addition to the implementation of the main task - the change of state power, is to plunge the state into a state of political chaos, or, as political technologists call it, - a state of "controlled chaos": "atomisation" of society, breaking social ties, imposing artificially Western individualism, i.e. creating a situation where state power is controlled by external management, and the country is in a state of chaos Based on this situation, we can conclude that traditional values of Kyrgyz society, which are capable of becoming a national idea, should act as an internal resource, and the maintenance of these values may well become the "soft power" that will unite the state and be transmitted outside the country, creating an attractive image of Kyrgyzstan. Such values may well be the cult of family, respect for age, honouring old age, and collectivism of Kyrgyz society. The high status of the institution of the family is characteristic of the Kyrgyz population, but is completely lost in the liberal society of the West. In addition, the collectivism of Kyrgyz society, characterised by collective rather than individual responsibility and a high level of social censure, is attractive. The family, tribe and clan are responsible for the actions of all their members and the misdemeanour of one person entails public censure of all members of the family. On the one hand, this demonstrates the absence of fair individual responsibility, but on the other hand, it contributes to the maintenance of a high moral and ethical level of each person who respects his or her clan. The Kyrgyz people have managed to preserve mythical thinking, however, not taking it to extremes, but adapting it to modern conditions, preserving ritual rules, such as the obligatory bowing to an elder in some regions, and getting rid of ancient prejudices. It is the preservation and transmission of such an identity that is quite capable of acting as a positive unifying idea of society, which can resist external influence.

Undoubtedly, in addition to ideological methods of neutralising external influence, it is necessary to toughen the criminal and legal liability of citizens and public associations for violation of public order, attempted unconstitutional seizure of power and related acts, to tighten control over the implementation of legislation in this area, and to hold the population accountable for these unlawful acts. For example, in the USA itself, the world centre of the struggle for democracy and human rights, a written or oral statement in a disloyal, blasphemous, rude or insulting tone about the form of state structure or the US Constitution, as well as about the US armed forces, is punishable by imprisonment for up to 20 years. It should be noted that the prosecutor's office and investigative bodies of the Kyrgyz Republic do not take the necessary initiative to identify illegal acts of NGO members engaged in anti-state activities and their further criminal prosecution.

However, priority should be given to ideological methods. As rightly noted by MGIMO professor A. Podberezkin, "there is a direct correlation between counteraction, even neutralisation of external influence in the form of "soft power" and ideology: the more attractive the national ideology and effective the ways of its influence, the more developed its basic provisions and arguments are for the nation, the less the society is susceptible to the influence of external instruments of "soft power"".[38]

Close relations with the Russian Federation can act as an external resource to counter the influence of third countries. Not every state can boast close cultural ties and a common historical past with a major regional and, in the long term, world power that is ready to co-operate, provide assistance and patronage on an almost gratuitous basis. The diplomatic bodies of the Russian Federation not only solve the tasks of providing mechanisms to prevent external influence on the internal state policy of the Russian Federation, but are also able to provide assistance in this counteraction to the allied states of the Russian Federation by providing assistance in monitoring the risks and threats of external influence, assessing the stability of political regimes, controlling the possibilities of political destabilisation, as well as implementing mechanisms of strategic mutual assistance to representatives of the authorities and elites.

In addition, the EAEU's common civilisational space may well become a guarantee of successful development of integration in the post-Soviet space and a factor of stability in international relations. It is the common Eurasian ideology based on the common traditional values of the peoples of Eurasia, common mentality and common historical past that can contribute to strengthening the security of the entire Eurasian space and the national security of each of the EAEU states individually, act as a tool for their civilisational modernisation, have a beneficial impact on the civilisational image of these states, increase their competitiveness against the transatlantic ideology of the West in the global world.[39]

Thus, accepting the fact that the modern foreign policy of the Western countries led by the United States of America represents external interference in the affairs of sovereign states,

---

[38] A. Podberezkin: There is a direct correlation between counteraction, even neutralisation of external influence in the form of "soft power" and ideology... // http://www.nasled.ru/?q=content/ a. podberezkin: There is a direct correlation between counteraction, even neutralisation of external influence in the form of soft power, and ideology.

[39] See: *Mishuchkov A.A.* Civilisation perspective of Eurasian integration / Bulletin of the Orenburg State University. - 2015. - №9 (184). - C. 10.

establishment of controlled governments, influence on the development of the political system, manipulation of the consciousness of the population, etc., we understand the need for adequate and timely counteraction to these processes. Political technologists and experts offer a large number of methods to counteract the technologies of external influence, but often the protective toolkit developed lags behind the modern reality or the protective mechanisms are not properly implemented. The Kyrgyz Republic is also hostage to the situation when programmes to counteract the mechanisms of external influence remain only programmes. Consequently, it is necessary to develop new ways of resisting external influence. Such mechanisms may well be the formation of a national idea based on traditional Kyrgyz values and close cooperation with the Russian Federation, both within the EAEU and in a bilateral format. Successful use of these resources can, if not rid Kyrgyzstan of the influence of a third state, at least minimise the negative consequences of this influence.

yes **I want** morebooks!

Buy your books fast and straightforward online - at one of world's fastest growing online book stores! Environmentally sound due to Print-on-Demand technologies.

Buy your books online at
www.morebooks.shop

Kaufen Sie Ihre Bücher schnell und unkompliziert online – auf einer der am schnellsten wachsenden Buchhandelsplattformen weltweit! Dank Print-On-Demand umwelt- und ressourcenschonend produziert.

Bücher schneller online kaufen
www.morebooks.shop

Printed by Books on Demand GmbH, Norderstedt / Germany